Dedicated to
Amelia Agyin-Birikorang.
May you find great joy in
the best news of all.

CHRISTMAS BIBLE VERSES TO REMEMBER

THE BEST NEWS OF ALL

SALLY MICHAEL

Illustrated by SENGSAVANE CHOUNRAMANY

New Growth Press, Greensboro, NC 27401

Cover/Interior illustrations: Sengsavane Chounramany
Art Direction and Typesetting: Dan Stelzer

ISBN: 978-1-64507-481-6 (paperback)

ISBN: 978-1-64507-482-3 (ebook)

Library of Congress Control Number: 2024941636

Printed in Canada

31 30 29 28 27 26 25 24 1 2 3 4 5

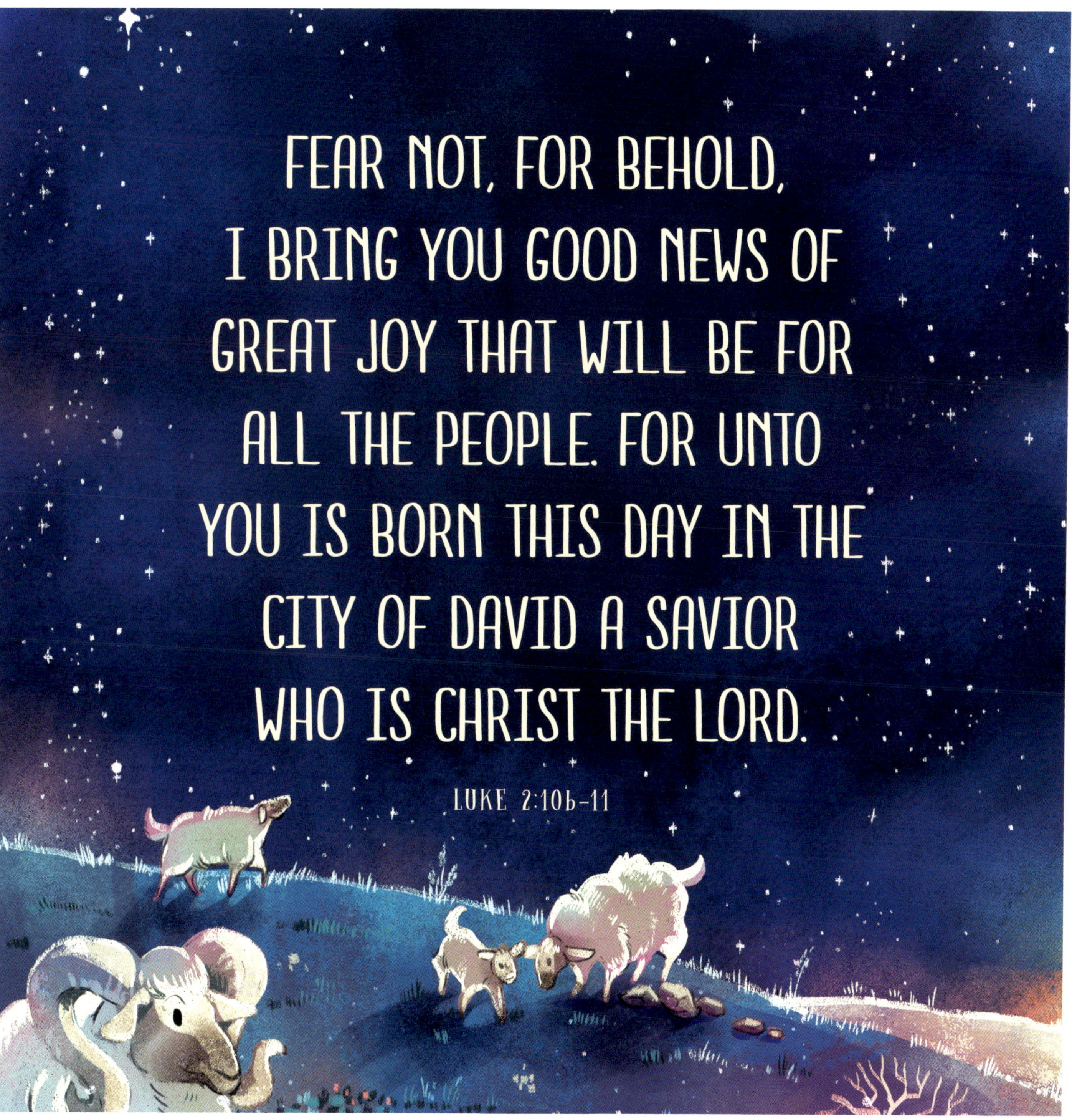
FEAR NOT, FOR BEHOLD,
I BRING YOU GOOD NEWS OF
GREAT JOY THAT WILL BE FOR
ALL THE PEOPLE. FOR UNTO
YOU IS BORN THIS DAY IN THE
CITY OF DAVID A SAVIOR
WHO IS CHRIST THE LORD.
LUKE 2:10b–11

What do you see when you look up in the sky?
The sun and clouds? You might see a bird or an airplane.

At night, you might see the moon and stars.

But what if you looked up and saw an elephant? Or a lion?

Would you be surprised, amazed...
and maybe even a little afraid?

One night long ago, some men were out in the fields watching their sheep when they saw something in the sky. It wasn't the moon or the stars. It was something very strange! Do you know what it was? It was an angel! Do you think they were surprised—and afraid—to see an angel?

Yes, they were surprised and afraid! The Bible says they were "filled with great fear."

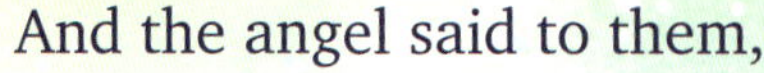

And the angel said to them,

"FEAR NOT, FOR BEHOLD, I BRING YOU GOOD NEWS OF GREAT JOY..."

The angel told them not to be afraid.
The angel said, "Behold! Look! See!
I am bringing you good news!"

Good news is about something wonderful!
What is some good news you have heard?

Maybe it was the news that you were going to grandma's house or, even better, that you were going to have a new baby in the family. Such good news!

But the angel's news was more than just good news.
It was good news of great joy!
It was the best news of all!!!

And the angel said to them,

"Fear not, for behold, I bring you
good news of great joy
THAT WILL BE FOR ALL THE PEOPLE."

This most wonderful news,
the best news of all was for

ALL PEOPLE...

... little children
and old grandmas,

busy farmers and
brave firefighters,

rich people
and poor people,

people who live near you,
and people who live in faraway places.

What was this most wonderful news?

"Fear not, for behold, I bring you good news of great joy that will be for all the people. FOR UNTO YOU IS BORN THIS DAY IN THE CITY OF DAVID A SAVIOR . . ."

King David had been born in Bethlehem. And now someone very special, more special than a king, was born in Bethlehem. He was someone who would be the Savior of all kinds of people, someone who would save simple shepherds and grand kings.

Who was this special baby?

". . . For unto you is born this day in the city of David a Savior, WHO IS CHRIST THE LORD."

Jesus, the Son of God, was born to be the Savior of all peoples.
He would take away the sins of everyone who would believe in him.
He would save them from punishment and bring them to heaven.

This is the greatest, best news of all! It's good news of great joy!

The shepherds heard the good news. But was this good news of great joy really true? Did God really send his own Son to save sinful people?

The angel told the shepherds how they could know it was true. "And this will be a sign for you; you will find a baby wrapped in swaddling cloths and lying in a manger."

Suddenly there were angels…

and more angels…

and more angels…

praising God and saying: “Glory to God in the highest
and on earth peace among those with whom he is pleased!”

Everywhere the shepherds looked,
they saw angels praising the greatness of God!
The sky was full of angels bringing good news of great joy!

God had sent his Son, Jesus!

When the angels left, the shepherds ran to find baby Jesus, the Savior of the world. They found Mary and Joseph. They found baby Jesus "wrapped in swaddling cloths and lying in a manger," just as the angel had said. And they knew the good news was true!

Then the shepherds praised God for being a great God! They thanked God for sending Jesus!

The good news of great joy is good news for you, too! Jesus can be your Savior! Do you want to praise and thank God for sending Jesus, the Savior, too?

"FEAR NOT, FOR BEHOLD, I BRING YOU GOOD NEWS OF GREAT JOY THAT WILL BE FOR ALL THE PEOPLE. FOR UNTO YOU IS BORN THIS DAY IN THE CITY OF DAVID A SAVIOR, WHO IS CHRIST THE LORD."

LIVING
BY THE
WORD

What can you do to remember the good news of great joy?

Learn the Christmas story. As a family, read and talk about the Christmas story from Luke 1:26–33; 2:1–20. Talk about why Jesus came as a baby, and what happened when Jesus grew up. Thank God for sending his Son.

Sing and tell the good news. Sing together the song "Go Tell it on the Mountain." Tell someone about Jesus being born to be the Savior.

Memorize Luke 2:10b–11: "Fear not, for behold, I bring you good news of great joy that will be for all the people. For unto you is born this day in the city of David a Savior, who is Christ the Lord."

Pray this prayer every day: *Teach me your way, O Lord that I may walk in your truth; unite my heart to fear your name (Psalm 86:11).* Pray that you will learn what the Bible says about God and his ways, that you will obey God's Word, and that God will give you a new heart.

Additional resources: *Good News of Great Joy*–book, Advent calendar and coloring book (available at Truth78.org)

PARENT NOTE

Children learn about God in baby steps—little steps of learning who he is, what he has done, and what he is doing now, plus little steps of obedience to his teaching and his ways. And, by God's grace, what they learn in little steps of trusting Jesus eventually grows into big steps of faith.

But children don't learn these things by themselves through their natural instincts. They learn them when they are taught the truths of God's Word. In Psalm 86:11, David humbly prays, "Teach me your way, O Lord." The ways of God are contrary to our sinful nature, which is why we must be taught by God (see also Proverbs 14:12 and Isaiah 55:8).

Teaching God's truth is necessary to lead children to obey the Lord from the heart. Children may obey God's commands simply because they like to please their parents or because it's expected of them. This can be a positive step, but it falls short of the kind of obedience that flows from personal conviction and love for God. Such conviction can only be brought about by teaching and the work of the Holy Spirit.

To come to saving faith, a child must embrace the whole of David's prayer in Psalm 86:11: "Teach me your way, O Lord, that I may walk in your truth; unite my heart to fear your name." Notice how he prays that the truth of God would affect his whole heart and life. Real, saving faith requires a change of heart. It requires embracing who God is and entrusting oneself completely to Jesus Christ.

God's Word can make your child "wise for salvation through faith in Christ Jesus" (2 Timothy 3:15). As you use God-breathed Scripture to teach, reprove, correct, and train your child in righteousness (2 Timothy 3:16), the Holy Spirit may chip away at your child's "heart of stone" and turn it into a "heart of flesh" (Ezekiel 36:26). Steps taken when little may lead your child to saving faith—to trusting in Jesus for the forgiveness of sin and the fulfillment of all his promises.

Your part as parent, grandparent, or other discipler of the next generation is to be a teacher, an example of walking in God's ways, and a model of a heart dedicated to God. May your prayer for yourself and your children each day be:

Teach me your way, O Lord,
that I may walk in your truth;
unite my heart to fear your name.
—Psalm 86:11

How to Use This Book

This book will encourage your child to trust Jesus and walk in his ways. The goal is to instruct their mind, engage their heart, and influence their will.

To Instruct the Mind

- Read the book several times.
- Explain any words or concepts unfamiliar to your child.
- Help your child to memorize the verse.

To Engage the Heart

- Interact with your child as you read the book. Dialogue about God and his ways. Help your child to see God's greatness and goodness. (See *Helping Children to Understand the Gospel* in the resource list.)
- Encourage your child to trust God in everyday events.
- Pray that your child would be receptive to the truth, trust Christ, and walk in his ways.
- Pray with your child that Jesus would give them a heart to love and glorify God.

To Influence the Will

- Talk with your child about ways to apply the verse in real-life situations.
- Encourage your child to act on what they have learned and to practice obedience to the truth.
- Guide your child in walking in the truth and living what they have learned.

Other Resources for Parents:

The Disciple-Making Parent: A Comprehensive Guidebook for Raising Your Children to Love and Follow Jesus by Chap Bettis

Gospel-Powered Parenting: How the Gospel Shapes and Transforms Parenting by William P. Farley

Helping Children to Understand the Gospel by Sally Michael, Jill Nelson, and Bud Burk

Instructing a Child's Heart by Tedd and Margy Tripp

Mothers, Disciplers of the Next Generation by Sally Michael

Reaching Your Child's Heart: A Practical Guide to Faithful Parenting by Juan and Jeanine Sanchez

Tips for Helping Young Children Memorize Scripture

Memorizing by repetition works well when teaching verses to young children:

1. **Say the reference.** First, clearly pronounce the reference. Then ask the child to repeat the reference. (You may want to explain that a reference is like an address that tells where to find a verse in the Bible.)

2. **Repeat the verse in sections.** Say the passage in several bite-sized sections, repeating each section with the child.

   For example:

   a. Parent: *In the beginning*; Parent and child: *In the beginning*

   b. Parent: *God created*; Parent and child: *God created*

   c. Parent: *the heavens and the earth*; Parent and child: *the heavens and the earth*

3. **Repeat the reference.**

4. **Review the verse** several more times lengthening the sections each time, giving the reference before and after the passage.

5. **Discuss the verse.** After the passage is memorized (usually in 3-4 repetitions), it is good to dissect it. Explain the meaning of unfamiliar words. Rephrase the passage and talk about how the verse applies to life.

Memory Verse Resources:

"Foundation Verse Cards." Verse cards for 2- to 5-year-olds in ESV or NIV. Truth78. https://www.truth78.org/foundation-verses-resources.

"Foundation Verse Coloring Book." Truth78.org

Fighter Verses. App for Apple or Android (includes Foundation Verses)

More in the Bible Verses to Remember series

Good Gifts Come from God helps children see all the good gifts God has given them and to remember James 1:17: "Every good gift and every perfect gift is from above."

Give God Your Worries helps children learn how God takes care of his creation and especially them and to remember 1 Peter 5:7, "Cast all your anxiety on him because he cares for you."

Our Great God helps children understand how great and good God is and to remember Psalm 95:3: "For the Lord is a great God, and a great King above all gods."